20 Costly Money Mistakes

ELIJAH O. OSENI

ISBN: 9798352565803

DEDICATION

This book is dedicated to everyone in the struggle trying to make ends meet.

CONTENTS

PREFACE

"Why money is difficult to make" was created as a result of research, education, and current events. The idea of money is prevalent and significant because it is a fundamental component of a source of livelihood.

Human reports, nevertheless, indicate that the sad story about it is that it's challenging to make. Although it may be simple for some, the goal of this book is to help readers understand why they have trouble making money.

CHAPTER ONE

MONEY

Money and her components

Money has a single context and the most common and shortest definition of money, as it appears in dictionaries and Britannica such is "a commodity accepted by general consent as a medium of economic exchange". One could add to the above definition the following: "money is a medium of exchange that allows people to obtain what they need to live". When it comes as standard pieces of gold, silver, copper, nickel, etc., stamped by government authority and used as a medium of exchange and measure of value, it is called hard money; money however, may be any paper note issued by a government or an authorized bank and used in the same way; when appearing as bank notes, it is called paper money. Money is also used as a preferred method of valuation: the price of a commodity of some kind is typically expressed in a set number of units of currency; this is the accepted value of money, accepted by both the buyer and the seller because the conventional value can also be used to buy other goods or services. It is not always necessary to utilize a monetary unit chosen as a value measure widely. For instance, during the colonial era in America, the Spanish peso served as the recognized means of commerce while the British pound served as the benchmark of value.

Why Money Exists?

Money exists because it demonstrated its effectiveness in economies that were centrally managed. Transactions of goods and services as well as the ongoing specialization of production are made possible by the presence of money and its roles as a unit of account and a measure of value. Trade would take the form of a direct exchange of one good for another in a barter-based economy where money was not utilized, just as it did among prehistoric peoples. It was a horribly complicated system, and the so-called "double coincidence of wants" was its fundamental flaw: In order to exchange tomatoes for shoes, for example, a farmer selling tomatoes who also needs a pair of new shoes would need to find a shoemaker who wants to buy tomatoes as well as come to some sort of agreement on what the tomatoes for shoes exchange rate should be, of course, depending on the relative prices of these two products. While bartering is still common in some parts of the world, money is increasingly seen as a more practical form of exchange that allows for more economic transactions. In a money economy, a producer or owner of a commodity may sell it for money that may be used to pay for more goods and services, saving them the time and energy needed to locate a potential buyer. Money is viewed as a cornerstone of daily life in our modern economic society, and this perspective is highly effective because: - it is recognized as a unit of account; - it is a widely recognized form of exchange; - it is simple to divide; - it can be durable and stable in terms of value;

When Did Money Appear?

Around 2,500 BC, the earliest records of the usage of money are found in Lydia's ancient kingdom as well as in Mesopotamia. (According to some historical texts, the Chinese invented coinage around the second millennium BC.) Here, money took the place of the barter system, which led to a true explosion in the variety of products available for trade. The majority of non-economic uses for money involved either traditional forms of exchange or ancient ceremonial rites with their lavish showy adornment. Trade in kind steadily increased, and some items tended to be chosen over others, primarily due to their capabilities as exchange mediums: Others were easily transportable and had high value densities, while some were robust and practical to store. Such items became widely valued, were simple to exchange, and eventually were accepted as money. Prior to the invention of coins and paper money (banknotes/American English bills), early types of money were used for bartering things. For instance, in ancient Asia Minor, metal cylinders of various sizes, metal disks in Tibet, and limestone disks in the Yap Islands were the first exchange items used as forms of primitive money. Other examples include rice or various small tools in China, cowrie shells in India, cocoa beans in Central America, dog's teeth in Papua New Guinea, quartz pebbles in Ghana, or gambling counters in Hong Kong. These items, which were initially accepted for specific trade activities alone, eventually shown their rising popularity and tended to be used for various non-economic uses and general trading use, successfully supplanting barter in the process. China is the country that is currently most largely acknowledged as the origin of paper currency (about AD 800). It was common practice in many ancient cultures to have laws that stated their set norms and demanded restitution for crimes or payment2 for brides; this was done to make up for the loss of a daughter's services to the head of the family. Rulers levied taxes or demanded tribute from their people, and religious authorities also prescribed the payment of taxes or various types of sacrifice (or offerings). This is how money emerged from deeply ingrained practices in prehistoric societies. Different types of money have evolved from the so-called commodity money, such as rice, cattle, and cowrie shells, which replaced the previous barter system. Hard money is made of precious metals, particularly gold and silver bars and ingots,5 or coins. Token money is made of other metals, like copper. Paper money or soft money, also known as representative money, is the type of money used today, like the banknotes (Amer. Eng. bills). Forms of fake money such bank deposits, treasury bills, bills of exchange, and credits that could be transferred by check quickly followed them. Modern innovations like the credit card and the check (American English check) serve most, if not all, of the traditional purposes of money.

TWO

THOSE WHO CAN MAKE MONEY

Money has undoubtedly provided both people and animals with a means of subsistence in the world of the twenty-first century.

Why I included animals may be a mystery to you. Feed for animals is purchased with money and is necessary for their survival.

Additionally, we need money to feed ourselves, to develop and become great, to manage our enterprises and firms, to support our children's education, and to take care of our families.

In essence, we can see that money is needed in all facets of life. Who among us is devoid of life? Absolutely no one!

FROM A CHILD'S PERSPECTIVE

As a child from age 0-18, there are only little ideas about making money one can have. This is as a result of child's inexposure to the real world, yet. However, it is stated that children from a poor background, if hardworking, starts making money around the age of 18.

When a child attain the age of 18, it is helpful that he starts thinking about making money by himself. This is a bitter truth this generation cannot afford to tell us. The parents owe a share of this duty, too.

FROM A REAL LIFE PERSPECTIVE

When I was younger, I was affected by some odd beliefs. I know most people were hypnotized with such beliefs, too. I was taught never to chase money. It was taken out from been a priority to life. "Just do well and be a good boy." they would say.

But as I grew up, I began to think about my life. "If I don't make money, how would I get to do with the issues of life?"

My needs were countless as the sands of the sea while my parents could only afford little out of my countless needs. Then, I knew I had to dissolve the thought and beliefs that has found its root in me. I had to learn how to make money by myself with the help of God.

As money is important in the issues of life, everyone who has life has to make money. You want to live a valuable and worthy life, make more money. As stated earlier, what we've come to live our lives for, needs money to be executed. Achievements require money.

Say to yourself, "I will make more money."

So, as far as money is important in the issues of life, everyone who exists at all should and must be able to make money.

THREE

THE FLEXIBILITY OF MONEY

FINANCIAL FLEXIBILITY

Being financially flexible means doing more with our money by following a monthly budget, being wise shoppers and taking advantage of employer-offered financial wellness tools and voluntary benefits such as financial counseling, student loan refinancing programs and employee purchase programs.

Money management can be stressful, especially if you've been trying to create a financial plan without help from a professional. With so many future life events to take into account — getting married, starting a family, buying a home, paying off your student loans, traveling, retiring and more — it can sometimes seem like you basically need to save every dime for future you with nothing leftover for the present.

Spending money is pretty much inevitable. And while there are many thoughts on how much you should have saved at every age, the race to build wealth can can make it hard to focus on the here and now. This is why it's important to have some financial flexibility.

Having financial flexibility doesn't mean loosening the reins and throwing caution to the wind when it comes to your money. It means striking a healthy balance between planning for today and the future, explains Ashley Russo, a financial advisor for Northwestern Mutual.

"You give yourself the freedom to enjoy life today without taking away from your future self," she says.

Is there such a thing as being too strict with your money?

Your future goals and current lifestyle can play a large part in how much money you have available to set aside for your dreams while also living life in the present. Someone who is paying rent and paying down student loans may have much less discretionary income compared to a person who is debt-free, doesn't have any kids and lives with their parents.

And as life goes on, both your income and your expenses may increase. You may have your own family to take care of, realize that you need to move from an apartment to a house, take care of an elderly parent and more. There are just so many life events that can change the way you've been planning — and sometimes, it's hard to afford it all and still save for your own future.

So when it comes to how strict you should be with your money, the answer is: It depends on your goals.

Not everyone needs to be as uncompromising with their saving as popular media — influencers, billionaires, financial websites — insists they should be. It all depends on your goals and how much time you have to reach them.

If you're 25 and want a modest retirement at 65, you'll be able to get away with saving less each month compared to someone who's 35 and wants to retire early or travel the world.

"There are some people who want to retire early. If that's truly your priority then you will have to save more aggressively compared to people who gave themselves a longer runway because they want to retire at 60 or 65," says Russo. "It all boils down to what your true wants are."

Not understanding what you truly want from your life could lead to undersaving or oversaving — aka not having enough money or having too much money. But even having too much money won't necessarily mean you're more satisfied with life if you missed important occasions and decided to say no to cherished events to save or earn extra money.

"We saw it in the pandemic," Russo says. "Although some people had extra money, it didn't mean they were any happier. There needs to be a balance between having money, saving money and spending money."

As humans, we want to have experiences with our money, she explains. So we need a balance between earning, saving and enjoying how we spend our income. But some people tend to put too much weight on one aspect over the others.

At the height of the Covid-19 pandemic, many people began limiting how they lived because of the financial uncertainty. Some people were afraid their assets would diminish and others were worried about getting laid off and not having any income to support themselves and their families. Others realized that it was time to make some serious changes in their money management habits.

"There are some people who are still not living life as they should because they aren't over [the pandemic]," says Brett Gersack, a senior wealth advisor at Halbert Hargrove.

How do you practice financial flexibility?

When it comes to figuring out how to strike that balance between spending money now and saving it for the future, you need to make a plan for how you want to use your money — aka, a budget.

"It all starts with the budget," Russo explains. "It's so hard to know where you're going if you don't know where you are. With a budget, you'll know how much you need for your expenses, how much you can afford to save and how much you have for other goals, like taking a trip or buying a house."

With a budget, you should factor in things you really care about — like traveling, dining out and celebrating birthdays. There are many platforms out there that can help you get started with a hassle-free budget, but the Mint app lets you connect your bank accounts, investment accounts, bills and credit cards so you can track everything in one convenient place. It will analyze your spending to help you create a visual breakdown of where your money goes. Plus, it can help you keep an eye on your **net worth.**

Honesty is the most important policy when it comes to budgeting. Overspending in a certain category can certainly be stressful. But if you notice a consistent pattern of spending more than you've allowed yourself for the same expenses, it could be a sign that you need to budget more to cover those costs.

Practicing conscious spending can also help you create a financial plan that strikes a balance between living your life now and saving for the future. Spending consciously means that you're purchasing the products or participating in experiences you really love while cutting out the costs for things you aren't actually interested in.

By cutting these expenses, you're freeing up cash that you can redirect toward your savings or other activities you enjoy. So maybe you love going to concerts but don't really watch TV; you might create a plan that allows you to stop paying for your streaming services so you can use that money to buy concert tickets and boost your retirement contributions.

FOUR
20 COSTLY MONEY MISTAKES

When you are starting out, you may make some less-than-stellar decisions regarding your finances.

But it's important to keep in mind that the choices you make today and the habits you form now can affect the rest of your financial life

Financial mistakes can be hard to bounce back from and can even take months or even years to fix. That's why avoiding costly money mistakes or credit mistakes can save you money, time and stress.

Check out the 20 costly money mistakes and how to avoid them

1. Using Credit Cards for Everyday Expenses

When you use your credit cards to cover the shortfalls in your spending, you can run up a huge amount of debt in a really short period of time. Plus, studies have shown that people tend to spend more money when they are paying with credit.[2] ☐

It's also easier to stop paying close attention to your budget when you constantly fall back on your credit card. You need to stop using your credit cards and start following a budget to kick your credit card habit.

2. Borrowing Money

When you are in a tight financial situation, you may be tempted to borrow money from your friends or your family. When you do this, you put a strain on your relationship with them. They may begin to question your financial decisions and feel like they can make comments about your spending habits.

They may also need the money back suddenly or you may feel guilty whenever you see them. It's a good rule of thumb to avoid loaning money to family or friends or risk damaging the relationship.

3. Quitting Your Job Without a Plan

When you quit your job, you do not qualify for unemployment insurance, and you may find yourself in a very tight financial situation. It is also more difficult to find a job when you are not currently employed.[3]

When you feel that your current employment situation is not good, you should begin looking for a new job right away. This will allow you to find a new job and prevent any gaps in your employment experience.

You may even decide to take a pay cut for your new job, but you will be secure in knowing that you have a job and a paycheck coming in.

4. Not Budgeting

When you do not have a budget, you do not have control of your finances. Failing to budget month after month means that you are not taking control of your financial situation.

Without a budget, you can make decent money and still struggle to get by. It can be difficult to reach your financial goals when you do not have a solid budget in place. Take the time now to set up a budget, and continue to do it every month. However, You can begin to make better financial decisions if you are budgeting and you know exactly where your money is going each month.

5. Not Having a Financial Plan

When you do not have a financial plan, you will not move forward to reach your financial goals. Your financial plan can help you make sure your spending matches your priorities.

Your financial plan will help you decide when you should start investing your money, how much to save for retirement, and other financial goals. Take the time to set up your financial plan today.

6. Not Setting Goals

Similar to a financial plan, your financial goals give you steps to work toward. These goals should be things like homeownership, starting your own business, retirement.

If you do not set specific goals, you will flounder. You may never get to the point where you have a down payment save for your home or be in a good position when it is time to retire. Take time to set solid financial goals and review them each year.

7. Going Without Insurance

Many people choose to go without insurance to save money. But this isn't a wise financial decision. That's because your car or health insurance is your safety net. It protects you in the event that you're in a major accident or have to deal with a serious health issue. In fact, one study found that 530,000 bankruptcies each year can be attributed to medical bills. Moreover, Make sure you have basic health insurance coverage, as well as car insurance. Keep in mind that many states require car insurance by law.

8. Making Financial Choices Out of Fear or Pressure

Another common mistake is to make a financial choice when you are afraid or you feel a lot of pressure to act right away. When you are afraid, you may not be considering all of the options, and you may end up making a costly mistake. It is important to take a step back and consider all of your options. You may also want to talk the decision over with someone you trust.

Another financial mistake is to give in to pressure to take a big financial step, like buying a new car to purchasing a home to getting married or having a child. You may not be ready for these steps and giving into pressure will not benefit you financially.

9. Getting Behind on Your Payments

When you fall behind on your house or car payments, you can create a cycle that is hard to break. You will end up paying late fees and other charges each time you fall behind. It may also damage your credit score, which can affect your finances in the future.[1]

The first thing you need to do is catch up on your late payments and then address any spending, budgeting or income issues that have caused you to fall behind. Then work to stick to your budget so this doesn't happen. again.

10. Paying Off Debt With Savings

You may be thinking that if your debt is costing 19% and your retirement account is making 7%, swapping the retirement for the debt means you will be pocketing the difference. But it's not that simple.

In addition to losing the power of compounding, it's very hard to pay back those retirement funds, and you could be hit with hefty fees. With the right mindset, borrowing from your retirement account can be a viable option, but even the most disciplined planners have a tough time placing money aside to rebuild these accounts.

When the debt gets paid off, the urgency to pay it back usually goes away. It will be very tempting to continue spending at the same pace, which means you could go back into debt again. If you are going to pay off debt with savings, you have to live like you still have a debt to pay—to your retirement fund.

11. Not Investing in Retirement

If you do not get your money working for you in the markets or through other income-producing investments, you may never be able to stop working. Making monthly contributions to designated retirement accounts is essential for a comfortable retirement.

Take advantage of tax-deferred retirement accounts and/or your employer-sponsored plan. Understand the time your investments will have to grow and how much risk you can tolerate. Consult a qualified financial advisor to match this with your goals if possible.

12. Excessive and Frivolous Spending

Great fortunes are often lost one dollar at a time. It may not seem like a big deal when you pick up that double-mocha cappuccino or have dinner out or order that pay-per-view movie, but every little item adds up.

Just $25 per week spent on dining out costs you $1,300 per year, which could go toward an extra credit card or auto payment or several extra payments. If you're enduring financial hardship, avoiding this mistake really matters—after all, if you're only a few dollars away from foreclosure or bankruptcy, every dollar will count more than ever.

13. Hiring the wrong financial adviser

It might sound crazy, but there are advisers out there that will push you toward expensive products that pay them big commissions but aren't good for you.

If you want to avoid being taken for a ride, make sure your advice is coming from a registered fiduciary, meaning they're required by law to act in your best interests.

These days, finding a trustworthy adviser has never been easier. With a free matching service called SmartAsset, you'll get be matched with up to three certified fiduciary advisers in five minutes.

Just take SmartAsset's adviser match quiz, review your pre-screened matches and speak with advisers, all at no cost to you.

If you're ready to be matched with local advisers that will help you achieve your financial goals, take this quiz now.

14. Not Understanding the Investment

One of the world's most successful investors, Warren Buffett, cautions against investing in companies whose business models you don't understand. The best way to avoid this is to build a diversified portfolio of exchange traded funds (ETFs) or mutual funds. If you do invest in individual stocks, make sure you thoroughly understand each company those stocks represent before you invest.

15. Letting Your Emotions Rule

Perhaps the number one killer of investment return is emotion. The axiom that fear and greed rule the market is true. Investors should not let fear or greed control their decisions. Instead, they should focus on the bigger picture. Stock market returns may deviate wildly over a shorter time frame, but, over the long term, historical returns tend to favor patient investors. In fact, over a 10 year time period the S&P 500 has delivered a 11.51% return as of May 13, 2022. Meanwhile the return year to date is -15.57%.

An investor ruled by emotion may see this type of negative return and panic sell, when in fact they probably would have been better off holding the investment for the long term. In fact, patient investors may benefit from the irrational decisions of other investors.

16. Telling Yourself Financial Lies

It's easy to tell yourself financial lies to make yourself feel better about the state of your bank account. Do you avoid looking at your bills or financial statements? Do you tell yourself that "future self" is going to take care your money woes?

We want to believe things will improve when we get a better job or a raise. The problem is, these financial lies cloud the reality of your money habits and the condition of your finances. Take an honest assessment of your finances and build on that.

17. Not Discussing Finances With Your Significant Other

It can be so awkward to talk about money with a significant other -- who wants to deal with that? But if you're getting serious with someone, it's time to have “the talk”

You can start by having general discussions on your views about money, how you deal with big purchases and how you invest and save. Have honest, open discussions about your views on money and work on coming up with financial goals together.

18. Substituting Growth For Money

This literary goes to the young adults. In your 20s, you are just starting your career. You will have many job offers with mouth-watering pay. It is only logical that you choose a job that offers growth instead of money, if you are interested in making more money in the future. You might want to start making enough money now, but in the long run, if you don't increase your value, you are going to remain in a spot.

19. Relying On Only One Source of Income

Have you ever stopped to ask yourself, 'what if I lose my job?' or 'what if this business crashes?' It is very risky to rely on only one source of income. You are most energetic in your 20s. therefore, it should be the time you take on different jobs to earn more money.

20. Keeping your money in too many places

One piece of repeated advice is not to put all your eggs in one basket. People sometimes interpret that to mean that they should be stashing money in all kinds of different accounts.

While it makes sense to keep your emergency fund in an account you don't check regularly, having your money in too many places means you could lose track and not know how you're progressing with your budget and savings. Simplify to keep track.

FIVE

HOW TO SUSTAIN MONEY AND CASH OVERFLOW

1. Lease, Don't Buy

Since leasing supplies, equipment, and real estate usually ends up being more expensive than buying, doing so may seem counterintuitive to someone who is only paying attention to the bottom line, or your income after expenses are paid off. But unless your company is flush with cash, you're going to want to maintain a cash stream for day-to-day operations.

By leasing, you pay in small increments, which helps improve cash flow. An added bonus is that lease payments are a business expense, and thereby can be written off on your taxes.

2. Use High-Interest Savings Accounts

This will provide you with liquidity while growing your cash position. The best high-yield savings accounts offer interest rates more than 17 times higher than the national average, meaning you'll earn more on the money you've stashed away.

3. Create A Budget

Business owners should sit down to thoughtfully estimate expected cash inflows and outflows. Factors that to consider include the sales cycle, terms and discounts provided customers, industry delinquency rates and other factors that may affect the timing of incoming cash. Similarly, it is necessary to estimate expenses and other cash outlays. This includes the timing of the purchase of equipment, raw materials and supplies. It also includes the schedule for payment of salaries, taxes and other day-to-day expenses. SCORE, a national nonprofit support group for small business owners, provides a free budget template that business owners can use to manage their cash flow.

4. Monitor The Result

Examining the budget should not be an infrequent activity. On at least a monthly basis (but more frequently if warranted), the actual cash flow should be compared with the budget to work out the kinks in the system. If cash inflows are less than anticipated, figure out the reason for the shortfall. If cash outflows end up being greater than expected, understanding the cause is also important.

Once the reasons for the budget variances are determined, the business can make the necessary corrections, either to the budget or the business plan or both.

5. Have A Plan B

Regardless of the amount of time and energy a business owner devotes to creating a budget, unexpected events can suddenly crop up, wreaking havoc on even the best cash-management system. During such times, the business might need to rely on a contingent source of cash to keep the operation running until things return to normal. Typical sources of contingent funding include lines of credit, personal assets and friends and family. Business owners should have a Plan B lined up well before the funds are needed. For example, a business owner who plans to borrow funds to cover a cash shortfall should have the loan or a line of credit in place well before the cash is needed. Allowing a cash-flow disruption to occur before applying for a loan is asking for trouble as most banks will hesitate to lend money to a business in distress.

SIX

CONCLUSION

In as much as it may take time and lot of effort to make money, certain factors has to be put in place to ensure the sustenance of the money made. After carefully analyzing the costly money mistakes buttressed in this book, I believe that a lot of lessons have been picked by acute senses of attentive listeners and readers who wouldn't just go by the book name but also the contents.

www.ingramcontent.com/pod-product-compliance
Lightning Source LLC
LaVergne TN
LVHW052114160826
845678LV00015B/3556

* 9 7 9 8 3 5 2 5 6 5 8 0 3 *